# ALICE'S PUZZLES THROUGH THE LOOKING GLASS

# AUTHOR'S NOTE

My thanks, first and always, to the former residents of Ein Helyg and 1 Derwendeg. You keep the monstrous crow at bay. For helping with the making of this book, I'd like to express my thundering gratitude to Hannah for listening to an unwise number of puns, and to Dani for the many years of useful head nods. Keep them coming or I'll starve.

Jason Ward, London, 2017

THIS IS A CARLTON BOOK

First published in Great Britain in 2016
This edition published in 2017 by Carlton Books
An imprint of the Carlton Publishing Group
20 Mortimer Street
London W1T 3JW

A CIP catalogue for this book is available from the British Library.

The publishers would like to thank Dover Books, iStockphoto and Shutterstock for their kind permission to reproduce the pictures in this book.

ISBN 978-1-78097-961-8

10 9 8 7 6 5 4 3 2 1

Printed in Dubai

# ALICE'S PUZZLES THROUGH THE LOOKING GLASS

A frabjous puzzle challenge, inspired by
Lewis Carroll's classic fantasy

Jason Ward

**CARLTON
BOOKS**

# CONTENTS

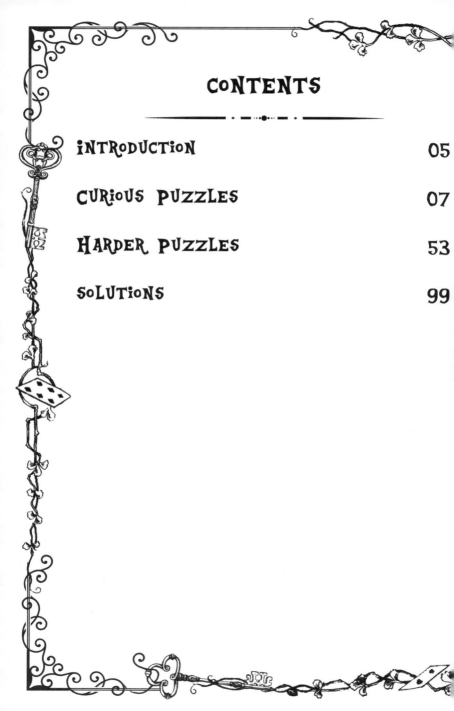

# INTRODUCTION

"Begin at the beginning," the King said, very gravely, "and go on till you come to the end: then stop."

The King of Hearts' advice to the White Rabbit is tremendously useful for most endeavours in life, from giving evidence in a tart-burglary trial to fixing a windmill, but becomes less useful when applied to puzzles. You can begin at the beginning, that's fine, but then what do you do? It's often the case that the solutions to the most satisfying problems are found not by assailing them head on, but coming in from another direction altogether.

Perhaps no-one understood this better than the Oxonian mathematics lecturer Charles Lutwidge Dodgson. Best known as Lewis Carroll, the author of *Alice's Adventures in Wonderland* and *Through the Looking-Glass*, the obsessive, inventive logician would lie in bed for hours every night trying to solve elaborate puzzles of his own devising. Some of those "Pillow Problems" can be found in this very collection, and like the rest of these riddles and conundrums – set in the world of Carroll's weirdly brilliant, brilliantly weird books – they aim to test skills of deduction, logical reasoning, arithmetic and, most importantly, creative thinking.

There are many different kinds of answers, but ultimately the questions can be approached in the same manner: begin at the beginning, find yourself in some place you didn't expect, and go on till you come to the end. Given the peculiar adventures of our young heroine Alice, this seems entirely appropriate.

# CURiOUS PUZZLES

# BISCUIT BUST UP

## "OH DON'T MIND US," said the Hatter.
### "We haven't quite finished our tea."
### "When did you begin?" asked Alice.
### "'Fourteenth of March, I think it was," he replied.

The March Hare was about to heartily disagree when he noticed the wicker tray cradled in Alice's arms.

"Pray, what tray is that?" said the March Hare.

"I've brought biscuits for your tea-party," explained Alice as she placed the tray onto the table. No sooner had she done this than the Hatter leaned across rattling teacups and commandeered the biscuits.

"You could have brought some cake, too," he grumbled between mouthfuls.

Before he was quite done, the Hatter ate half of the biscuits on the tray plus half of another biscuit. Sensing his chance, the March Hare grabbed the tray next and ate half of what was left plus half a biscuit, too. The pair slumped into a gluttonous lull and the Dormouse, rousing from its slumber, ate half of the remainder plus half a biscuit before promptly returning to sleep. Alice looked at the desert of crumbs before her and gloomily ate the final biscuit.

How many biscuits were on the tray when Alice arrived at the tea-party?

Solution on page **100**

# OYSTERLiNGS

**THE WALRUS** and the Carpenter were walking under the sulkily shining moon when they came across an Oyster and his seven Oysterlings.

"Are your young Oysters male or female?" asked the Carpenter. The eldest Oyster winked his eye and shook his heavy head. "Half of them are male," he replied.

How is this possible?

Solution on page **100**

# DISEMBODIED VERSE

## THE GRIN OF THE CHESHIRE CAT was
### the first thing Alice spotted, floating above
### the bough of a tree.

"Well! I've often seen a cat without a grin," she thought; "but a grin without a cat!"

The Cat didn't bother to wait for the rest of its body to appear fully before sharing its riddle with Alice:

> "My first, you hear its sullen roar
> When wandering by the ocean's shore.
> My second in the gambler's art
> Hath played no mean or paltry part,
> But, fired with sordid thirst to win,
>   It often aids him in his sin.
> My whole is something that is found
>   Upon the face of all around,
> Yet if you take from me my face,
>   I sound a title commonplace."
> "Do you know what I am?" asked the Cat

Solution on page **101**

# AGAINST ALL ADVICE

**THE GOAT** pushed his spectacles up the bridge of his very long nose. "Say," he said, "does this journey seem at all unusual to you?"

Alice looked around the carriage. The Horse was gnawing on one of the seats. "Why do you ask?" she replied.

"I told a man the other morning that I had to catch the 12:50 train," the Goat explained, "and he vigorously warned me against it. I can't think what he meant."

Why did the man advise the Goat not to take the train?

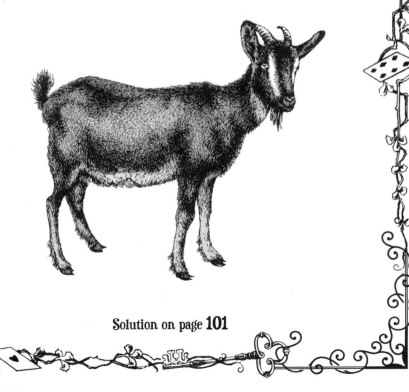

Solution on page **101**

# ENTOMOLOGICAL EQUATIONS

**THE GNAT** was certainly very large:
"about the size of a chicken," Alice thought.

She had found herself sitting quietly under a tree, while the Gnat was balancing itself on a twig just over her head, and fanning her with its wings. It was pointing out all of the insects around them:

All but two of the insects were Rocking-horse-flies
(which live on sap and sawdust).

All but two of the insects were Snap-dragon-flies
(which live on frumenty and mince-pie).

All but two of the insects were Bread-and-butter-flies
(which live on weak tea with cream in it).

Including the Gnat, how many insects was Alice looking at?

Solution on page **102**

# FUSSY FELINE

## THREE SISTERS at breakfast were feeding the cat,

The first gave it sole – Puss was grateful for that.

The next gave it salmon – which Puss thought a treat.

The third gave it herring – which Puss wouldn't eat.

Explain the conduct of the cat.

From the magazine *Puzzles from Wonderland* by Lewis Carroll

Solution on page 102

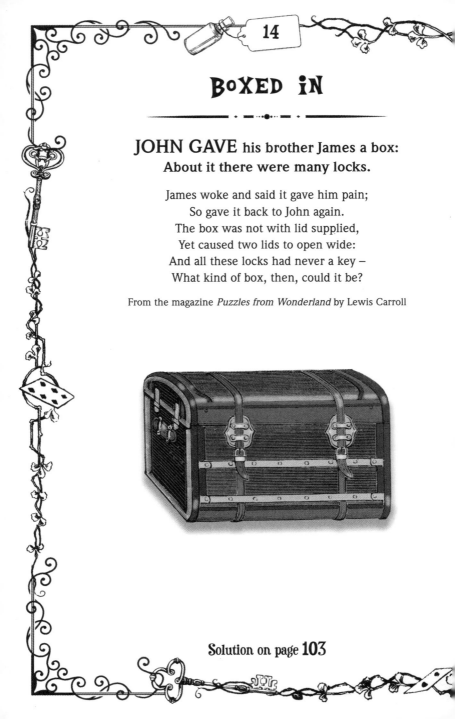

# BoXED iN

**JOHN GAVE his brother James a box:**
**About it there were many locks.**

James woke and said it gave him pain;
So gave it back to John again.
The box was not with lid supplied,
Yet caused two lids to open wide:
And all these locks had never a key –
What kind of box, then, could it be?

From the magazine *Puzzles from Wonderland* by Lewis Carroll

Solution on page 103

# NOT THE QUIET CARRIAGE

## "I DON'T BELONG TO THIS RAILWAY JOURNEY AT ALL," said Alice.
### "I was in a wood just now – and I wish I could get back there!"

The other passengers took little notice of Alice's plight. "I am three times older than the Goat," the gentleman dressed in white paper said aloud, to no-one in particular.

He nodded over at his travelling companion, who had shut his eyes again.

"I must be getting younger, too, because five years ago I was five times older than him!"

How old is the gentleman dressed in white paper?

Solution on page 103

# FiSH SUPPER

**"AS TO FISHES,"** the Red Queen said, putting her mouth close to Alice's ear, "her White Majesty knows a lovely riddle – all in poetry – all about fishes. Shall she repeat it?"

"Please do," Alice said very politely.

The White Queen laughed with delight, and stroked Alice's cheek. Then she began:

"'First, the fish must be caught.'

That is easy: a baby, I think, could have caught it.

'Next, the fish must be bought.'

That is easy: a penny, I think, would have bought it.

'Now cook me the fish!'

That is easy, and will not take more than a minute.

'Let it lie in a dish!'

That is easy, because it already is in it.

'Bring it here! Let me sup!'

It is easy to set such a dish on the table.

'Take the dish-cover up!'

Ah, that is so hard that I fear I'm unable!

For it holds it like glue –

Holds the lid to the dish, while it lies in the middle:

Which is easiest to do,

Un-dish-cover the fish, or dishcover the riddle?"

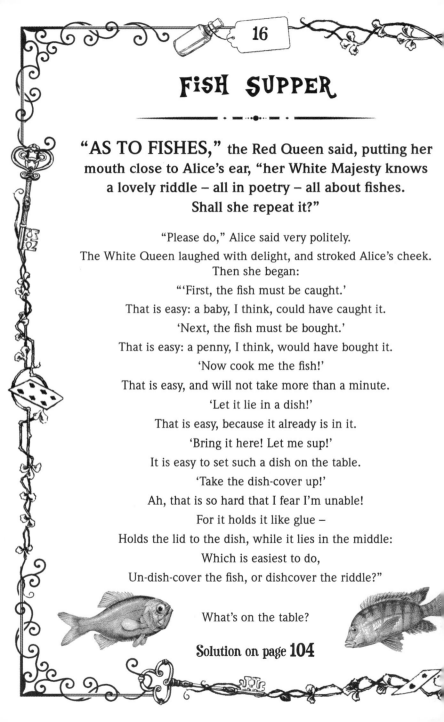

What's on the table?

**Solution on page 104**

# TWO RIDDLES

## WITH THIEVES I CONSORT,

With the vilest, in short,
I'm quite at my ease in depravity;
Yet all divines use me,
And savants can't lose me,
For I am the centre of gravity.

What am I?

## MY HEAD AND TAIL both equal are,

My middle slender as a bee.
Whether I stand on head or heel
Is quite the same to you or me.
But if my head should be cut off,
The matter's true, though passing strange,
Directly I to nothing change.

What am I?

Solution on page **104**

# DOWN IN THE HOLE

### "TWEEDLEDUM AND TWEEDLEDEE
**Agreed to have a battle;
For Tweedledum said Tweedledee
Had spoiled his nice new rattle."**

In the middle of their tussle, as Tweedledum was hitting everything within reach (whether he could see it or not), he accidentally knocked Tweedledee into a deep hole.

"You're going to struggle to get out of there. Nohow!" said Tweedledum.

"Contrariwise," replied Tweedledee, "this is going to take a great deal of time."

At the end of the day, Tweedledee had only climbed four feet. The hole, he reckoned, was twelve feet deep. It rained during the night as he slept, and he was swept down three feet. With Tweedledum watching helplessly, the same pattern repeated itself daily: up four feet during the day, down three feet during the night.

How many days was Tweedledee in the hole?

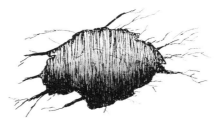

Solution on page **104**

# BUSHEL BUSINESS

## DREAMING OF APPLES ON A WALL,
### And dreaming often, dear,
### I dreamed that, if I counted all,
### – How many would appear?

From the magazine *Puzzles from Wonderland* by Lewis Carroll

Solution on page **105**

# THE SNEEZING SALESMAN

**THE COOK** used so much pepper in her soups that she had to buy it from a special merchant, who travelled from door to door with sacks full of peppercorn and an imposing pepper mill.

Instead of payment, as a toll the merchant kept a tenth of all the pepper he ground. How much pepper did he grind for the Cook, who had just one sack after the toll had been taken?

Solution on page 105

# PULLiNG THE OTHER ONE

## THE LION AND THE UNICORN

were done with fighting for the day; the crown would
still be there tomorrow. Seeking diversion and all out
of plum cake, they decided to play tug-of-war
with Hatta and Haigh instead.

Although it was difficult, the Lion could just about out-pull the
Unicorn and Hatta together. The Lion and the Unicorn together could
just hold Haigh and Hatta, neither pair being able to budge the other.
If Hatta changed places with the Unicorn, however, then Haigh
and the Unicorn won with ease.

How did the four rank in terms of strength?

Solution on page 106

# AN AVERAGE FROG FAMILY

**"I SHALL SIT HERE,"** the Frog-Footman said, "on and off, for days and days." He was sitting on the ground near the door, staring stupidly up into the sky.

"But what am I to do?" said Alice. "Anything you like," the Footman replied, and began whistling. "He's perfectly idiotic!" she thought.

The whistling quickly started to bother Alice, and so she decided to distract him. She asked him how old he was.

"How can anyone remember such a thing?" the Footman said. "I do know that my brother is two years older than I am, and my sister was born four years before he was. My mother was 28 when I was born and the average age of all of us is 39."

"He seems to be able to remember everything but his age!" Alice thought. "There's no use in talking to him."

How old was the Frog-Footman?

Solution on page **106**

# A QUEENLY SUM

**THE RED QUEEN** and the White Queen
sat close to Alice, one on each side. "You can't be
a Queen, you know, till you've passed the proper
examination," said the Red Queen. "And the
sooner we begin it, the better."

"Can you do Addition?" the White Queen asked. "What's one and
one and one and one and one and one and one and one and one
and one?"

"I don't know," said Alice. "I lost count."

"She can't do Addition," the Red Queen interrupted. "Can you do
Division? Divide a loaf by a knife – what's the answer to that?"

"I suppose –" Alice was beginning, but the Red Queen answered for
her. "Bread-and-butter, of course. Try a Multiplication sum. What's
five times four times three times two times one times nothing times
one times two times three times four times five?"

Alice considered it for a moment. "Oh, I know how to solve that!"
she replied eagerly.

What answer did she give?

Solution on page 107

# DEAR DAIRY

**IT WAS ALWAYS TEA-TIME** at the March Hare's house, which meant there was always tea.

Neither the March Hare nor the Hatter ever gave the matter any thought – and the Dormouse was usually dozing – but their constant tea drinking also required constant milk. The tea-party demanded so much milk, in fact, that there was a small field of cows whose sole purpose was keeping the milk jug full.

This field, behind the house of the March Hare, contained black and brown cows. Four black and three brown cows gave as much milk in five days as three black cows and five brown cows gave in four days.

Which kind of cow was the better milker?

Solution on page **107**

# FELINE FRUSTRATION

**THIS CLASSIC** "verse charade" riddle is
Lewis Carroll's earliest known puzzle.

A monument – men all agree –
Am I in all sincerity,
Half-cat, half-hindrance made.
If head and tail removed should be,
Then most of all you strengthen me;
Replace my head, the stand you see
On which my tail is laid.
What is it?

Solution on page **108**

# A FACE-DOWN HAND

## "THE QUEEN! THE QUEEN!"

**called out the Five of Hearts, and Alice watched three playing cards fling themselves to the ground.**

First came ten soldiers, followed by ten courtiers, followed by ten royal children, followed by ten guests, followed by the White Rabbit, followed by the Knave of Hearts, followed, finally finally finally, by the King and Queen of Hearts.

The procession stopped in front of Alice. "What's your name, child?" the Queen demanded.

"My name is Alice, so please your majesty."

"And who are these?" said the Queen, pointing to the three cards lying around the rose-tree. She could not tell whether they were gardeners, or soldiers, or courtiers, or three of her own children.

Alice didn't have any more of an idea than the Queen, but wanted to be polite. She heard a timid cough at her side. The Rabbit raised himself upon tiptoe, put his mouth close to Alice's ear, and whispered:

"There is a Diamond to the right of a Club, a King to the right of a Knave, a Knave to the left of a Knave and a Diamond to the left of a Diamond."

What are the three cards?

Solution on page **108**

# A Good Egg

## THE EGGS WERE LIKE HOT CAKES.
### Out of all of the curious items for sale in her shop, the Sheep found that eggs were the most popular.

Seeking to take advantage of this, the Sheep took a certain number of eggs to market and sold them. The next day the number of eggs left over had doubled, but she sold the same amount. On the third day, the new remainder was trebled, and again she sold the same number as before. On the fourth day, the remainder was quadrupled but her sales were still the same. On the fifth and final day, what had been left over had quintupled and she still sold exactly the same amount of eggs. This meant that she was now left with no eggs at all.

What is the smallest number of eggs the Sheep could have taken to market the first day, and how many did she sell daily?

Solution on page 109

# PUTTING THEMSELVES TOGETHER

**ALICE IN ALL HER LIFE** had never seen soldiers so uncertain on their feet: they were always tripping over something or other, and whenever one went down, several more always fell over him, so that the ground was soon covered with little heaps of men.

It seemed to be a regular rule that, whenever a horse stumbled, the rider fell off instantly. From her safe hiding spot behind a tree, Alice watched thirteen of the dazed, hopeless riders stumble about before mounting the first available steed.

What is the probability that exactly twelve of the riders managed to somehow find their own horse?

Solution on page **109**

# LAWN FOR LUNCH

## IT WASN'T THE GARDEN'S FAULT
that it looked plain. Sitting next to a garden abloom
with talking flowers, almost any plot of land would be.

The farmer of the garden didn't have the time to trim the grass
himself and so left the job to his livestock. He found that his cow
and goat would eat all of the grass in forty-five days, the cow and the
goose would eat it in sixty days and the goat and the goose would eat
it in ninety days.

Assuming that the grass is no longer growing, if the farmer left
the cow, goat and goose in the garden together how long would it
take them to eat all of it?

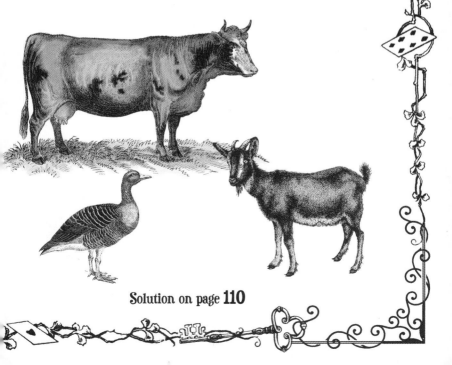

Solution on page **110**

# TIME TO REFLECT

## THE LOOKING GLASS WAS MELTING AWAY, just like a bright silvery mist.
In another moment Alice was through the glass, and had jumped lightly down into the Looking Glass Room. "They don't keep this room so tidy as the other," she thought to herself.

Alice began looking about, and was pleased to find that there was a real fire in the fireplace, blazing away as brightly as the one she had left behind. The clock on the chimney-piece was still there, too, but everything about it was completely reversed. Despite being the exact opposite to the one in her own house, however, the looking glass clock displayed exactly the same time.

All of the hours on the clock face were indicated by the same mark, and both hands were the same in length and form. It had been between 6 and 7 o'clock when Alice had passed through the glass.

What was the time to the nearest second?

From a puzzle by Lewis Carroll

Solution on page **110**

# CATERING CONUNDRUM

**TRAYS AND TRAYS AND TRAYS** of white
and brown bread sat all around Haigh and Hatta.
When they weren't distracting each other – which was
often – the pair were busy preparing refreshments
for the fight between the Lion and the Unicorn.

Haigh could fill a tray with twenty pieces of bread in five minutes.
Hatta might have been able to work at the same speed, but he had
a cup of tea to attend to, so it would take him ten minutes to fill a
tray with the same amount.

How long would it take
Haigh and Hatta to fill a tray
with twenty pieces of white
and brown bread if they
worked together?

Solution on page 111

# A Moving Quarry

**THE LONG, LOW HALL** was lit up by a row of lamps hanging from the roof. Alice was heading towards the passage into the loveliest garden you ever saw when she heard the pattering of feet: a hundred yards behind her was the White Rabbit.

"Oh my ears and whiskers, how late it's getting!" it said to itself, taking a watch out of its waistcoat pocket. Alice turned around and walked towards it, but after a hundred yards the Rabbit was still the same distance away.

Can you explain why?

Solution on page **111**

# A REGAL RUNAROUND

**SOMEHOW OR OTHER,** they began to run.
Alice never could quite make out, in thinking it over
afterwards, how it was that they started: all she
remembers is, that they were running hand in hand,
and the Red Queen went so fast that it was all
she could do to keep up with her.

Before she knew it, the Looking Glass House had disappeared from view. "Faster!" cried the Queen. "Or we'll never get to the Garden of Live Flowers! Here, you see, it takes all the running you can do, to keep in the same place."

After seven miles, Alice and the Red Queen ran past the White Queen, who had set out at the same time to walk from the Garden of Live Flowers to the Looking Glass House. When each reached their destination, they immediately turned around and headed back the way they came.

On the return journey, they passed each other ten miles from the Garden of Live Flowers. Both the White Queen and the Red Queen with Alice travelled at the same relative speeds throughout their journey.

What's the distance between the Looking Glass House and the Garden of Live Flowers?

Solution on page 112

# OUT OF TIME

**"OH! WON'T SHE BE SAVAGE** if I've kept her waiting! Oh! The Duchess, the Duchess!" The White Rabbit was muttering to himself, a pair of white kid-gloves in one hand and a pocket-watch in the other.

Alice looked at the face of the watch and announced the time as it appeared to her. This seemed to shake the Rabbit from his stupor, for he turned to her and said, "You seem to be unfamiliar with my much-improved timepiece.

"The minute hand," he explained, with palpable satisfaction, "always moves in the opposite direction to the hour hand. Except for this, the watch is precisely the same as any you might be accustomed to."

The hands of the Rabbit's watch were exactly together between the hours of four and five o'clock, and they started together at noon.

What was the real time?

Solution on page **112**

# ABSENT HEDGEHOGS

**THE CROQUET GAME WAS IN PIECES.** The soldiers had doubled themselves up to make the arches and the players all had their flamingoes to use as mallets, but the hedgehogs were nowhere to be seen.

"Someone didn't bring the hedgehogs," the Queen of Hearts roared. "Off with their head!" The Queen's argument was that, if something wasn't done about it in less than no time, she'd have everybody executed, all around.

The gardeners looked at each other nervously.

Two said, "It wasn't me, it was Seven."

Seven said, "Two didn't do it, Three did."

Three said, "Seven didn't do it, I did."

Five said, "Three didn't do it, Two did."

Each gardener made one truthful statement and told one lie. Who had forgotten to bring the hedgehogs?

Solution on page 113

# UNDER THE SEA

**THE MOCK TURTLE** sat sad and lonely on a little ledge of rock, sighing as if his heart would break. He was reminiscing, as he often did, about his school in the sea.

Other than the Lobster-Quadrille, the Turtle's favourite part of his school days was the actual school itself. The institution was made up of three buildings, each 1,000 feet high (or deep, depending on where you're standing).

One of the buildings was shaped like a pyramid, one looked like the top half of a sphere and the other was a perfect cylinder. Also, on the outside of each building was a path leading from its base to its top, which would climb one vertical foot for every fifty horizontal feet.

If the Mock Turtle ever managed to return to his beloved school and wanted to travel the shortest distance from base to top, which building should he visit?

Solution on page 113

# BRANDY BOTHER

## FRIENDS OF LEWIS CARROLL
would recall in later years how he liked to
surprise them with puzzles he'd devised.
This was one of his favourites.

There are two tumblers: one contains fifty spoonfuls of pure brandy and the other contains fifty spoonfuls of pure water.

Take one spoonful of brandy from the first tumbler and transfer it to the second, stirring it up afterwards. Then take a spoonful of mixture from the second tumbler and transfer it to the first.

Has more brandy been transferred from the first tumbler to the second, or has more water been transferred from the second tumbler to the first?

Solution on page **114**

# FULL LEISURELY WE GLIDE

**THE WHITE KING** had wanted to send all of his horses and all of his men to put Humpty Dumpty back together again, but he could only find twelve of the men, and none of the horses.

He stood with his men on the left bank of a river, confused. "I could have sworn this was a brook yesterday," he muttered.

Luckily for his party, Tweedledum and Tweedledee had gone for a trip down the river in their rowboat and were happy to help out. The boat could carry Tweedledum and Tweedledee safely but only one soldier at a time, not even a soldier and either a Dum or a Dee.

After much head scratching, the King managed to get himself and his twelve soldiers from the left bank of the river to the right bank while leaving Tweedledum and Tweedledee with their boat. How many times did the boat cross the river?

Solution on page 114

# RoYALLY AFRaiD

**UNYIELDING FEAR** can do strange things to a gardener. To distract himself from his ever-present worry about a sudden visit from the Queen, the Five of Hearts had started to make up riddles. He told his latest one to his fellow gardeners as they painted the rose-trees again:

> If I were to ask the Queen and the chair
> Both to tell me what they were,
> And then should beg of you to bear
> To the top of the house the Queen and her chair,
> The Queen, her chair, and yourself, all three,
> In the very same sentence would answer me.

> What's the answer to Five's riddle?

Solution on page **115**

# FOOTLOOSE FOOTMAN

**AS THE FISH-FOOTMAN** put on his livery
for the day ahead, he thought about the new contract
he had just agreed with the royal household.
He was relieved that the King had negotiated the terms
himself – such matters were usually the concern
of the Queen, who took the notion of executing
a contract all too literally.

The new agreement stated that the Footman would be paid £8 a day
for thirty days on the condition that he would additionally have to
forfeit £10 for every day that he idled. The poor steward had been
looking forward to what he would do with all of
his extra money, but at the end of the
thirty days he discovered that neither
he nor the royal household owed
the other anything.

How many days of work
did the Fish-Footman
put in and on how
many did he idle?

Solution on page 115

# TiME TRADES

"**ALL WRONG!**" sighed the Hatter.
"I told you butter wouldn't suit the works."
The March Hare looked at his watch gloomily:
then he dipped it into his cup of tea, and
looked at it again. "It was the best butter,
you know," he meekly replied.

Alice had been looking over his shoulder with some curiosity. "What a funny watch!" she remarked. "It gains a minute every hour."

"Oh, that's nothing!" said the Hatter. "Mine loses a minute every hour!"

The March Hare nodded solemnly. "We set them both to the correct time at eight o'clock on Wednesday morning, though."

Taking care to wipe off the tea, Alice compared the two watches. "How strange! There's a difference of exactly one hour in the time they're showing."

When's the tea-party taking place?

Solution on page **116**

# MISSING OUT

**IN HIS LIFETIME,** Lewis Carroll wrote
nearly 100,000 letters. Many of them contained
puzzles, such as this one, sent to Mary,
Ina and Harriet "Hartie" Watson.

When . a . y and I . a told . a . . ie they'd seen a

Small . . ea . u . e with . i . . . , dressed in crimson and blue,

. a . . ie cried " 'Twas a . ai . y! Why, I . a and . a .y,

I *should* have been happy if I had been you!"

Said .a.y "You wouldn't." Said I . a "You shouldn't –

Since *you* can't be *us*, and *we* couldn't be *you*.

You are *one*, my dear . a . . ie, but *we* are a . a . . y,

And a . i . . . e . i . tells us that
*one* isn't *two*."

Solution on page **116**

# SEEING RED (OR GREY)

**IT WAS BAD ENOUGH** when Alice had
to pass through the wood where things had no names.
Now, as she looked from trunk to leaf and from
leaf to sky, she realized that she was entirely
unable to tell one colour from another.

The sky was getting darker, or perhaps it was getting lighter. "What a thing... something that is!" she thought. "And how fast it comes! Why, I do believe it's got wings!"

Alice saw that it was either a Bishop or a Castle, but she couldn't say for sure, nor whether it was Red or White. She remembered someone somewhere telling her something. Who, where and what, however, was unclear.

The information came back to her as the figure approached:

*White Castles always tell the truth, Red Castles always lie, Red Bishops always tell the truth, and White Bishops always lie.*

It now stood in front of Alice, and said: "I am not a Bishop."

The figure cleared its throat. It spoke again: "Also, I am either Red or White."

What's the identity of the figure?

Solution on page **117**

# THE WILLIAMS

### THE LAST TIME HE COUNTED,
**Father William had three children:
Noah, Arthur and John.**

The combined ages of the three children was half of Father William's. Five years later, during which time Joyce was born, Father William's age equalled the total of all of his children's ages.

A decade has since passed, with Phyllis appearing during that interval When Phyllis was born, Noah was as old as John and Joyce together.

The combined ages of all of the children is now double Father William's age, which is only equal to that of Noah and Arthur together Noah's age also equals that of the two daughters together.

What are the current ages of Father William and all of his children?

Solution on page 117

# COUNTING SHEEP

**ALICE RUBBED HER EYES,** and looked again. She was in a little dark shop, leaning with her elbows on the counter, and opposite to her was an old Sheep, sitting in an arm-chair, knitting.

The shop seemed to be full of all manner of curious things, but Alice's eye was drawn to the shelf that contained five jars of sweets.

"There are so many sweets in those jars!" Alice exclaimed. "Have you ever counted them?"

The Sheep looked at Alice over a great pair of spectacles. "I do little else, child."

This was actually true. The Sheep had worked out that four of the jars contained a total of 220 sweets. The fifth jar contained 20 fewer than the average of all of them.

How many sweets did the fifth jar contain?

Solution on page **118**

# WHiFFLiNG THRoUGH THE TULGEY WooD

**THE POOR KNIGHT** certainly *was not* a good rider.

As he had a habit of doing, the Knight tumbled off his horse. He had been galloping through the woods at a pace of nine miles an hour. Although it didn't say anything, obviously, his horse – who was usually very patient indeed – refused to carry on without a proper saddle that wasn't loaded with bunches of carrots, and fire-irons, and many other things.

Chastened, the Knight walked back at a rate of three miles an hour. He found that he arrived at his stable exactly eight hours after he had originally set out.

How far into the woods had he left the horse?

Solution on page 118

# SECOND GUESSING

## "HAVE YOU GUESSED THE RIDDLE YET?" the Hatter said.

"No, I give it up," Alice replied. She didn't know why a raven is like a writing-desk. Perhaps it had something to do with them both producing notes, she thought, but that didn't seem quite right. "What's the answer?"

"I haven't the slightest idea," said the Hatter.

Alice sighed wearily. "I think you might do something better with the time," she said, "than wasting it in asking riddles that have no answers."

"Well, here's one that does have an answer," said the Hatter. "What is that from which you may take away the whole and yet have some left?"

Solution on page **119**

# PENAL PUZZLE

**HATTA WAS IN PRISON,** waiting for his trial and an opportunity to actually commit the crime he was being punished for.

The only things the guards gave him for sustenance were some oyster shells, a pen and this puzzle:

Connect all twelve points with five straight lines, without raising the pencil or going through any point twice. The lines can cross each other, but you must end on the first point to produce a closed circuit.

How did Hatta complete the puzzle?

Solution on page **119**

# MiDWAY ON HER JOURNEY

## ALICE FOUND HERSELF IN DARK WOODS, the right road lost.

A finger-post stood at each of the three paths ahead of her.

The first path's finger-post read: "You should not come this way."

The second path's finger-post read: "This is the path to take, or else the third path is the correct one."

The third path's finger-post read: "The monstrous crow is waiting on the first path." At least one of the signs is false.

Which path should Alice follow?

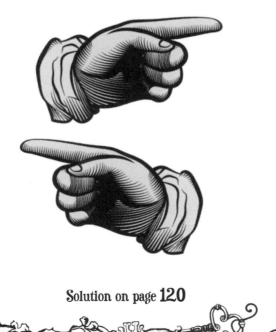

Solution on page 120

# WiNE NoT?

## THE GUESTS AT THE FEAST
### had been singing for some time.
### Hundreds of voices joined in the song's final chorus:

> "Then fill up the glasses with treacle and ink,
> Or anything else that is pleasant to drink:
> Mix sand with the cider, and wool with the wine –
> And welcome Queen Alice with ninety-times-nine!"
> "Ninety times nine makes eight hundred and ten,"

Alice thought to herself, "I wonder if anyone's counting."

They weren't: the Red Queen, the White Queen and the White Knight had each brought seven casks of wine to the feast.

At the end of the night, as the animals, birds and flowers shuffled out of the large hall, they saw that seven were empty, seven were half full and seven were untouched. The two Queens and the Knight wanted to share these out fairly so that each of the three could take an equal share of wine and casks.

How did they accomplish this without any measuring devices except for the casks themselves?

Solution on page **120**

# YOLKFOLK

## "NOW, TAKE A GOOD LOOK AT ME!"
said Humpty Dumpty. "I'm one that has spoken to
a King, I am: mayhap you'll never see such another:
and, to show you I'm not proud, you may shake
hands with me!"

In addition to fraternizing with royalty and balancing precariously
on the top of high, narrow walls, Humpty Dumpty was also a father
to two oval-shaped children: Daisy, the elder, and Denzil, who was
the younger.

Whenever anyone asked their ages, Humpty Dumpty would reply that
eighteen more than the sum of their ages is double the age of Daisy,
while the age of Denzil is six less than the difference of their ages.

How old are Daisy and Denzil?

Solution on page 120

# HARDER PUZZLES

# Something to Dunk

**IT IS QUITE IMPOSSIBLE** for a person
to drink as much tea as the Hatter and not develop
a tremendous predilection for biscuits.

Accordingly, every week the Hatter bought eight packets of twenty
biscuits. He would devour these with such carelessness, however,
that he could never eat an entire biscuit: there would inevitably be
an end left over from each one.

To try to save money, he kept these uneaten ends to squish into more
biscuits. From four ends, rather cunningly, he could make one entirely
new biscuit.

How many biscuits did the Hatter eat every week, including those
made up from the ends of others?

Solution on page 121

# DISCRIMINATING DESCENDANTS

## IF HE'D SPENT LESS TIME STANDING ON HIS HEAD and more time at the kitchen table, Father William might have prevented his children from being such fussy eaters.

For the governess of Father William's brood, dinnertime was a distinct ordeal: seven of the children wouldn't eat spinach, six wouldn't touch carrots, and five wouldn't eat beans. Four would eat neither carrots nor spinach, three would touch neither spinach nor beans, and two wouldn't eat carrots or beans. One of the children wouldn't eat spinach, carrots or beans. And not a single child would eat all three of the vegetables.

How many children did Father William have?

Solution on page 121

# A FAWN FEIGNING INTEREST

## "WHAT DO YOU CALL YOURSELF?"
### the Fawn asked Alice.

"I wish I knew!" thought poor Alice, for she had forgotten. She answered, rather sadly, "Nothing, just now."

They walked on together through the wood, but trying to make conversation with a stranger is challenging when you're a stranger to yourself, too. "Do you know any riddles?" asked the Fawn, in what seemed more like a polite gesture than a genuine question.

Alice thought it would be disconcerting if she remembered some riddles and not her own name, but as she didn't want to embarrass her new friend, she contrived to make something up on the spot.

"Yes!" she replied. "What word starts with 'e', and ends with 'e', but often has only one letter in it?"

What's the answer to Alice's riddle?

Solution on page 122

# LIKE A FRIEND

## TWEEDLEDUM AND TWEEDLEDEE
were arguing again. It hadn't quite gotten to fisticuffs, but they still had time: dinner was hours away yet.

"I have twice as many friends as you do. Nohow!" said Tweedledum.

"Contrariwise," replied Tweedledee, "I have twice as many friends as you."

How can they both be right?

Solution on page 122

# RUNNING UP THAT HILL

—————— • —••• • ——————

## "I SHOULD SEE THAT GARDEN FAR BETTER," said Alice to herself, "if I could get to the top of that hill."

The journey, as ever, was less straightforward than expected. In fact, it was somewhat backforward. After finding herself returning to the Looking Glass House several times, Alice finally made it to the bottom of the hill. She climbed to the summit at a rate of one and a half miles an hour, stopping at the top to look out at the curious country before her: the ground divided into squares by brooks and green hedges, just like a large chess-board. The descent, meanwhile, was understandably far swifter, and she came down at a rate of four and a half miles per hour.

Excluding the time she spent on the hilltop, it took Alice six hours to make the journey up and down.

How far was it to the top of the hill?

Solution on page 123

# LEAVING THE NEST

### "UGH, SERPENT!" said the Pigeon.

"But I'm not a serpent, I tell you!" said Alice. "I'm a little girl."

"A likely story indeed!" said the Pigeon, in a tone of the deepest contempt. "I've seen a good many little girls in my time, but never one with such a neck as that. And you're not even little!"

"That's just because I'm bigger than you," said Alice, who was always ready for a brisk argument. "I can assure you that I am a little girl."

"Well, how old are you then?" the Pigeon demanded.

"Oh dear, how puzzling it all is!" Alice thought. It was a complicated question at the best of times, and these certainly were not that.

"I was six on my last birthday and I'll be eight on my next birthday."

How was this possible?

Solution on page 123

# SUNLESS SARTORIAL SELECTIONS

**THE KING OF HEARTS** was dressing in the dark again. His efforts were an attempt to avoid waking the Queen as, like everyone in the royal household, he was terrified of incurring her wrath.

In the King's sock drawer were seven pairs of red socks, four pairs of white socks, three pairs of black socks and one pair of blue socks.

What is the least number of socks the King needs to remove from the drawer to ensure that he will have at least one matching pair?

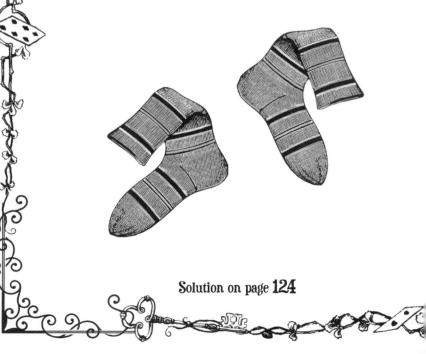

Solution on page **124**

# Nᵒ BALL GAMES

**BILL THE LIZARD** was taking a break
from jury duty and being stuffed down chimneys
to play with his favourite ball.

After several minutes during which he just sat quietly and stared at
the ball, the Lizard threw it.

The ball travelled a short distance, came to a complete stop, reversed
direction and came back the opposite way. He didn't hit or bounce
the ball, or tie anything to it.

What did Bill do?

Solution on page **124**

# RECIPROCAL ZUGZWANG

## THE RED KNIGHT and the
### White Knight were fighting for Alice.

The foes were observing the Rules of Battle. What exactly these were was unclear to Alice. "One Rule seems to be, that if one Knight hits the other, he knocks him off his horse; and, if he misses, he tumbles off himself. Another Rule seems to be that they hold their clubs with their arms, as if they were Punch and Judy. What a noise they make when they tumble!"

A new round was about to start. If the White Knight fell off his own horse then he would have won the same number of rounds as the Red Knight, but if he knocked his opponent off his horse then he would have won twice as many rounds as the Red Knight.

How many rounds had each Knight won prior to the start of this round?

Solution on page 125

# ON THE PAYROLL

## THE HOURS WERE LONG AND CONFUSING, but at least the King paid well. Or Hatta and Haigh assumed that he paid well: they couldn't quite figure it out for sure.

When the pair had been hired by the King as his Messengers, they had each been offered two different salary options. Hatta chose the first option: a beginning salary of £300 a year with increases of £60 each year. Haigh selected the other option: a beginning salary of £150 every six months and an increase of £30 every half-year.

Which of the two Messengers chose the better deal?

Solution on page 125

# SEA LEGS

## THE CATERPILLAR put the hookah into its mouth, and breathed in deeply.

Alice waited patiently until it chose to speak. In a minute or two the Caterpillar took the hookah out, yawned once or twice, and shook itself.

"A ship is anchored in port," the Caterpillar said, "and a ladder hangs over its side."

Alice wondered if the creature was making some kind of analogy. It went on:

"The ladder's bottom rung grazes the water. Between each rung is a distance of 40cm, and the length of the entire ladder is 320cm. If the tide rises at a rate of 25cm per hour, how long will it take for the water to reach the top rung?"

"This almost definitely isn't an analogy," thought Alice to herself sadly.

What's the answer to the Caterpillar's question?

Solution on page 126

# FiELD SURGERY

**"WHO ON EARTH** were they fighting?"
the King's Doctor asked. He surveyed the
wood in dismay: the ground was blanketed with
injured soldiers. "Oh, they weren't fighting anyone,"
replied the King. "They're just a little unsteady
on their feet."

The King informed the Doctor that exactly
two-thirds of the men had received a black eye,
three-fourths had sprained a wrist
and four-fifths had stubbed a toe.

"It follows, then," the Doctor surmised,
"that at least twenty-six of the men
have a black eye, a sprained wrist
and a stubbed toe."

How many injured men
were in the wood?

Solution on page **126**

# DRAUGHTY CONDITIONS

**THE TRAIN PASSENGERS** were tutting in the way that train passengers tend to do. "I'm sorry about this," said the Guard, putting his head in at the window. "We don't have any leaves on the line."

"Isn't that a good thing?" Alice asked the Guard, who had already left.

"Of course it isn't! How else is the train supposed to move without any kindling?" said the gentleman dressed in white paper, who at that very moment was starting to worry that his fellow passengers would soon realize he was covered in the stuff.

Without waiting to be asked, the Goat pulled out the draughts set that he kept on his person at all times in case of unexpected logistical difficulties. "I'm a draughtsman," he announced to a carriage that did not appreciate his joke.

Alice, the Beetle, the Horse and the gentleman dressed in white paper agreed to play with the Goat to distract themselves; by the time someone from the rail company arrived with sacks filled with leaves, everyone had played everyone else once.

How many games of draughts were played?

Solution on page **127**

# FAiRLY REDiSTRiBUTED WEALTH

## FATHER WILLIAM'S BROTHER – who for reasons no-one quite understood was also called Father William – had a dozen children.

Frustrated by their father's inconsistent pocket money allocations, his nine boys and three girls agreed to share their pennies equally.

Every boy gave an equal sum to every girl, and every girl gave another equal sum to every boy. Each child then possessed exactly the same amount.

What was the smallest possible amount that each child then possessed?

Solution on page 127

# i AM THE EGG MAN

## INEVITABLY, THE WORST HAPPENED:
**Humpty Dumpty had a great fall. With a dimming sense of hope the army marched towards the imperilled egg.**

"He had it coming," the King thought to himself, but a promise was a promise all the same. He'd assured Humpty Dumpty – with his very own mouth – that in the event of a wall-related misfortune he'd send all of his horses and all of his men. If only he hadn't forgotten that he had quite so many of both.

Inspecting the men and horses was an exhausting feat for the King, given that the army was forty miles long. Nevertheless, he galloped from the rear of his troops to the front and then back again, during which time the army advanced forty miles.

How far did the King travel?

Solution on page 128

# i AM THE WALRUS

**"O WOEFUL, weeping Walrus, your tears are all a sham! You're greedier for oysters than children are for jam."**

The rhyme had been going around and around in the Walrus' head for so long that he hadn't noticed it appear, nor did he know the origin. It was a Friday, and over the past five days he had eagerly devoured thirty whole oysters. Each day he had eaten three more oysters than the day before, sobbing all the while.

How many oysters did the Walrus eat on Monday?

Solution on page **128**

# PiLLOW PROBLEMS

**THE DIARIES** of Lewis Carroll abound
with word-based riddles and mathematical
puzzles that he would devise and then try
to solve as he lay awake at night.

Below is his entry from 20th June 1892. Can you work it out?

*Invented what I think is a new kind of riddle: "A Russian had three sons. The first, named Rab, became a lawyer; the second, Ymra, became a soldier. The third became a sailor: what was his name?"*

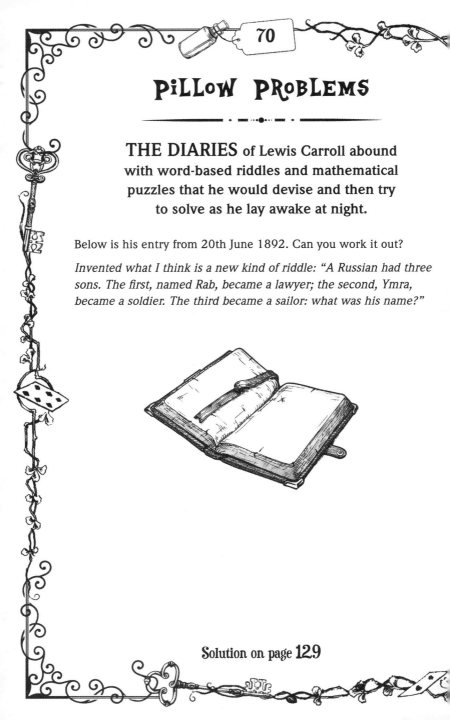

Solution on page 129

# UNFORTUNATELY, A JURY OF PEERS

**CONSIDERING HOW OFTEN the**
Queen of Hearts accused her subjects of crimes,
it's unsurprising that the court of justice got through
jurors like the Knave (allegedly) got through tarts.

By this point, there were only thirty creatures left who were still
eligible to be jurors, most of whom were rather dim. The system for
being called up was about as simple as the royal court got: a barrel
was filled with enough parchment scrolls for every eligible juror, two
of which contained a summons. The creatures then took it in turns to
remove scrolls, and the two who pulled out a summons would then
join the existing jury members (the jury would lose two members a
day, usually to officers of the court placing them into canvas bags and
sitting on them...)

Does Bill the Lizard have a better chance
of not becoming a juror if he goes first,
or if he goes tenth, after one
summons has already
been taken?

Solution on page 129

# SALT iRE

## "NONSENSE!" said the Sheep.
## "Why would I need to label items I sell in my shop?"

"So that your customers could know what they were buying?" replied Alice.

"They can just ask me, if they're so insistent."

"What are these, then?" Alice asked, pointing at a shelf carrying a dozen unlabelled sacks.

The Sheep looked at the girl as if she had said something stupid.

"Those are items I sell in my shop."

After many more minutes of confused, convoluted conversation, the Sheep finally explained to Alice that eleven of the sacks contained sugar and one contained salt. Unsurprisingly, it had little idea which was which, and even less interest in the answer.

This was somewhat helpful, at least: Alice had wanted to buy three sacks of sugar. Also, she remembered someone telling her once that salt weighed slightly more, a fact that she had found incredibly boring until that exact instant.

With a single use of the shop's large weighing scales, how could Alice be sure she bought three sacks of sugar?

Solution on page 130

# o UNFRABJOUS DAY!

## HE DIDN'T WANT TO BE IMPOLITE,
**but the beamish boy who slew the Jabberwock had
expected a more conventional reward for his labours.**

As he rested again by the Tumtum tree, standing in uffish thought,
the local Almoner had approached him; he had the distinct facial
expression that a person wears when they no longer have to worry
about a Jabberwock whiffling through a tulgey wood and ruining their
Tuesday. You know the look.

The Almoner sat on the ground before the boy and unfolded a strip of
velvet. Upon the velvet were some coins: one made from gold,
one made from silver, and a third made from bronze.

"To receive one of these coins, you must make one true statement,"
the Almoner said in a tone not nearly apologetic enough for the boy's
liking. "If what you say is false, you will receive nothing."

What did the boy say to guarantee that he received the gold coin?

Solution on page **130**

# IMPROPER WAGON MAINTENANCE

---•--•••—■—•—•---

## THE HORSES WERE REVOLTING.

They could only express this with a swish of a tail, of course, but the message was clear: they would no longer attend to Humpty Dumpty if he kept on insisting on sitting on such high, narrow walls.

Almost as if to prove their point, Humpty Dumpty required another rescue during the negotiations. The King's stop-gap measure for this was to load up his foot-soldiers into wagons, with each wagon carrying the same number of soldiers.

Halfway to the wall, ten of the wagons broke down, and so it was necessary for each remaining wagon to carry one extra soldier.

After finding they couldn't put Humpty back together again, the troops set out for home, but they realized that fifteen more wagons could not be used. The soldiers from these wagons were loaded into the functional wagons, and so each wagon contained three more soldiers than when they had started out.

How many soldiers had the King sent?

Solution on page 131

# RACE FOR THE PRIZE

**THE ANIMALS** had enjoyed the Caucus-race
so much that they'd agreed to make it a weekly
occurrence, whether they were dripping wet or not.
Occasionally if it had rained, some of them would dab
themselves with a puddle, but it wasn't the same.

As they took the races more seriously they became less fun – the
Mouse had tried to warn them but they accused him of being a
miserabilist.

Halfway through the most recent race, the Dodo was a certain
distance behind the Eaglet, and the Lory was twice that distance in
front of the Eaglet. Each competitor ran at their own uniform rate of
speed, with the result being that the Dodo passed the Eaglet in seven
minutes and passed the Lory five minutes later.

In how many minutes after the Dodo would the Eaglet pass the Lory?

Solution on page **131**

# TROUBLE AND A HALF

### "I'M SO SORRY," said Alice.
### "Please could you repeat that?"

Humpty Dumpty looked at her as if he were addressing a particularly slow-witted child. It was not something she enjoyed.

"It isn't complicated," he sighed dramatically. "If a hen and a half lays an egg and a half in a day and a half, how many and a half who lay better by half will lay half a score and a half in a week and a half?"

Alice's gaze had drifted down to the wall. "I'm so sorry," she said. "Please could you..."

What was the answer to Humpty Dumpty's question?

Solution on page 132

# OKAY AT CROQUET

**THE ROYAL COURT** seemed to grow larger by the day. The reason for this, of course, was that it did. How else would the Queen have enough courtiers to berate?

In the latest batch of ill-fated recruits were four cards: Five, Two, Four and Six. The roles they held – not necessarily respectively – were Pantler, Doorward, Cup-Bearer and Dapifer. When they weren't working or being threatened, they loved to play croquet. This was difficult, given that they had to take turns as the arches, but they didn't let it dampen the fun.

After a few weeks, several facts became apparent. Both the Dapifer and the Pantler were better croquet players than the Doorward. Although the Pantler consistently trounced him, the Cup-Bearer wouldn't play with anyone else. Four played a worse game than Two. Four and Six had adjoining quarters and often played together in the evening. The Doorward lived near the Cup-Bearer, but none of the others.

What court role did each card hold?

Solution on page 132

# THERE GOES THE SUN

**ALICE WAS BEGINNING** to get very
tired of sitting by her sister on the bank,
and of having nothing to do.

The hot day made her feel very sleepy and stupid, and she could
barely remember how long it had been since the summer holidays had
begun. Despite the sudden heat, the weather had been inconsistent,
without nearly the number of golden afternoons she'd hoped for.

It had rained on thirteen days, although whenever it rained in the
morning the afternoon was fine, and every rainy afternoon had
been preceded by a fine morning. In total there had been eleven
fine mornings and twelve fine afternoons. Alice was discounting the
current day in this tally, as it was clear that nothing of any interest
was going to happen on this riverbank.

How many days had the summer holidays been going on for?

Solution on page 133

# CURSED BE LOVE!

**THIS MYSTERIOUS POEM** is alleged to have been written by Lewis Carroll for the brother of a woman called Lady Ure. Can you guess what is so unusual about it?

> I often wondered when I cursed,
> Often feared where I would be –
> Wondered where she'd yield her love,
> When I yield, so will she.
> I would her will be pitied!
> Cursed be love! She pitied me…

Solution on page 133

# CRUEL AND UNUSUAL PUNISHMENTS

· — ··•·· — ·

**THE JUDICIAL SYSTEM** of the Looking Glass world left a lot to be desired. Perhaps this was to be expected in a world that was entirely backwards.

The latest recipient of such careless justice was poor Hatta, who was in prison being punished ahead of the start of his trial. Usually, Hatta's gaoler brought him a supper of oyster-shells, but one evening – it was unclear whether this was out of compassion or boredom – he brought two large jars instead.

The gaoler explained that this was a chance of freedom. One of the jars contained 100 red marbles and the other contained 100 white marbles, and Hatta was free to redistribute them however he wished between the two. When he was finished the jars would be shaken thoroughly, he would be blindfolded and then presented with one of the jars at random. At this point, if Hatta pulled a red marble out of the jar he would be released. If he selected a white one he would have to stay indefinitely, or at least until the gaoler got bored and/or compassionate again.

How should Hatta distribute the marbles to have the best chance of being set free?

Solution on page 134

# GUEST AT THE FEAST

## THE SENSATION of surprise was indistinguishable from disappointment. Alice saw that the banquet had started without her.

She glanced nervously along the table as she walked up the large hall. There were all kinds of guests: some were animals, some birds, and there were even a few flowers among them.

Despite their many differences in size, shape and ability to photosynthesize, every two guests shared a dish for soup, every three shared a dish for fish, and every four shared a dish for mutton. Alice counted 65 dishes on the table altogether.

How many guests attended the banquet?

Solution on page 134

# INTERGENERATIONAL CRAB CATCHING

## "CAN YOU ROW?" the Sheep asked, handing Alice a pair of knitting needles.

"Yes, a little – but not on land – and not with needles –" Alice was beginning to say, when suddenly the needles turned into oars in her hands, and she found they were in a little boat, gliding along between banks: so there was nothing for it but to do her best.

"Feather! Feather!" the Sheep cried again, taking more needles. "You'll be catching a crab directly."

"A dear little crab!" thought Alice. "I should like that."

She looked over to the next boat along, where a group were indeed catching crabs. After some polite conversation – not helped by the Sheep's constant bleating – Alice learned that in the boat were two fathers and their two sons, and that they had each caught one crab to take home with them.

Alice peered over the neighbouring boat's gunwale: the bucket they were using contained only three crabs.

How could this be?

Solution on page 135

# A Piece of Cake

**"HAND ROUND the plum-cake, Monster,"**
the Lion said, lying down and putting his chin on
his paws. "And sit down, both of you" (to the King and
the Unicorn): "fair play with the cake, you know!"

Alice seated herself on the bank of a little brook, with the great dish
on her knees, ready to saw away diligently with the knife. The round
plum-cake was intended to be divided
among Alice, the King, the Lion,
the Unicorn, Hatta, Haigh and
two of the King's hungriest men.

How did Alice give everyone
some cake by only making
three straight cuts with the
knife, and without moving
any of the pieces?

Solution on page 135

# WITHOUT A FULL DECK

**THE AGED AGED MAN** and the White Knight
were playing cards. Given that the old man refused
to stop a-sitting on a gate, this wasn't as easy
as the Knight had hoped.

The game they played – the Knight's own invention, he claimed – was
simple. Arguably it wasn't even a proper game. Each man had a deck
of 52 cards, and to win they needed to pull two aces at random from
their deck in their first two draws.

The aged aged man said that if he drew an ace on his first turn then
he would return it to the pack for his second turn, while the Knight
declared that if he drew an ace on his first turn he would put it aside
and then take his second turn.

Remarkably, both men did indeed draw an ace from their deck on
their first turn. Which one had the better chance of winning the
whole game?

Solution on page 136

# A Lying Leporine

**THE CHIMNEYS** were shaped like ears
and the roof was thatched with fur. It had to
be the house of the March Hare.

Alice had chosen to visit because she reasoned that, as it was
May, the Hare wouldn't be raving mad, or at least not as mad
as it was in March.

On this matter she was wrong. While the Hare was completely
sane on Mondays and Tuesdays, on Wednesdays and Thursdays it
believed all true propositions to be false and all false propositions
to be true. Muddying the pot of tea further, on Mondays and
Wednesdays the Hare was completely truthful and said what it really
believed, while on Tuesdays and Thursdays it always stated the
opposite of what it believed.

Don't worry, it gets worse: on Monday and Tuesday afternoons
the Hare hosted tea-parties, while on Wednesday and Thursday
afternoons it went to tea-parties instead. On Fridays, Saturdays and
Sundays it chose to stay in bed, drink tea and eat cake, not speaking
to anyone at all.

Not surprisingly given her circumstances, when Alice saw the
March Hare she didn't know what day of the week it was. What
single yes or no question could she ask to find out what the
Hare was doing that day?

Solution on page 136

# PASTRY PREMONITIONS

## THE QUEEN WAS THINKING GIDDILY
### about lawn sports and retribution when the Four of Hearts burst into her private study.

"Off with his head!" she demanded, before realizing she was alone with her nightwatchman and there was no-one else to hear. "Off with your head! Take it off, right now!"

After being chased around the room for several minutes, Four eventually persuaded his irate employer to put down the chair she'd been wielding. He explained his unauthorized visit: the previous night he had dreamt that someone would try to steal her tarts. The premonition shook the monarch to the point that she didn't even notice Four bolt from the room in terror.

The Queen spent that day glaring at her tarts from a turret. Sure enough, the Knave tried to steal them. After this, he also tried to escape from the guard who sat on him. He failed in both pursuits.

That evening, Four was summoned before the Queen, but instead of the commendation he was expecting, she ordered his beheading (to take place as soon as the executioner was done with the Knave and most other members of her court).

Why did the Queen react this way?

Solution on page 137

# OUT ON THE TILES

## "PERHAPS LOOKING GLASS MILK
isn't good to drink," Alice thought. She tiptoed
through the house and into the kitchen, wanting
to find out for sure.

Inside the room Alice found no milk on the kitchen table nor, for that matter, a kitchen table on the kitchen floor. This was disappointing but meant that she could survey the floor's gleaming black-and-white tiles. They made up a rectangle across the room, comprised of squares: 93 tiles on one dimension and 231 on the other.

With the soot of the fireplace still on her shoe, Alice traced a line from one corner of the kitchen to its opposite. How many tiles did the soot line cross?

Solution on page 137

# AN EVOLUTIONARY CUL-DE-SAC

**"CRAWLING** at your feet," said the Gnat,
"you may observe a Bread-and-butter-fly.
Its wings are thin slices of bread-and-butter,
its body is a crust, and its head is a lump of sugar."

"And what does it live on?" Alice asked.

"Weak tea with cream in it."

A new difficulty came into Alice's head. "Supposing it couldn't find any?" she suggested.

"Then it would die, of course."

"But that must happen very often," she remarked thoughtfully.

"It always happens," said the Gnat.

For now, however, the area was abuzz with the poor little creatures. The Bread-and-butter-flies were 25 per cent of the number of other insects in the wood.

What percentage of the insects in the wood were Bread-and-butter-flies?

Solution on page **138**

# SOMEBODY KILLED SOMETHING

**BEAMISH** was not the word that the boy
would have chosen to describe his current temperament.
He was decidedly unbeamish.

It was clear that there would be no galumphing back. His vorpal
sword was broken; it wouldn't snicker-snack. As the Jabberwock
advanced, burbling as it came, the boy tried to think of an alternative
strategy. If he couldn't defeat his manxome foe with might, he would
have to use logic instead.

"Imagine a barber," the boy screamed into the gathering dark. "This
barber shaves everyone in his town who doesn't shave themselves,
and never shaves anyone who does shave themselves."

It was difficult to tell if the Jabberwock was listening, but its leathery
wings started to beat a little slower.

"This is a problem, obviously, when it comes to the barber's own
personal grooming. If he shaves himself, he's violating the rule by
shaving someone who shaves themselves. If he doesn't shave himself,
he's also violating his rule by not shaving someone who doesn't shave
themselves. So what should the barber do?"

The Jabberwock scrunched up its fishy face. First it stopped dead
in its tracks, and then it plain dropped dead. O frabjous day!
Callooh! Callay!

What's the answer to the boy's riddle, and how did it slay the
Jabberwock?

Solution on page 138

# A FLIPPER WITH A HAND

**SILENCE FELL** upon the Walrus and the Carpenter. It was as if they had both immediately fallen asleep, except they had not.

That night the old friends had already spoken of so many things: of shoes – and ships – and sealing-wax – of cabbages – and kings – and why the sea is boiling hot – and whether pigs have wings. What else was there to say?

To stave off the hush they decided to try a card game, with a stake of one penny for each hand played. When a sudden peckishness forced the end of the game, one had won three hands and the other had won three pennies.

How many hands did the Walrus and the Carpenter play?

Solution on page 139

# BLiND CHANCE

**"OH! THE FLAMINGOES** have flown away, as I said they would," the Queen of Hearts cried.

No-one at the croquet ground could remember the Queen making this prediction, but they were united in their relief that at least she wasn't threatening anyone.

Without mallets – even those of the wading bird variety – to play with, the game couldn't continue, and so the cards headed indoors. A new game was devised by the Queen herself: four blindfolded cards would stand in different corners of a room before being brought to the room's centre, whereupon they would be spun around and asked to take turns finding their way back to their original corner. Once a corner was occupied it became off bounds.

The Queen added that anyone who failed to find their own corner would be executed, which the players decided to assume was a joke, against all evidence to the contrary.

What is the probability that all four cards would return to their original corners?

Solution on page 139

# TUMTUM TREE TROUBLES

**"DON'T YOU THINK** there's something strange about this tree?" the Red Queen asked the Red King. It wasn't a sentence she had anticipated ever saying aloud to another person, but there it was anyway.

True to somnolent form, the King didn't respond; he just continued to lie crumpled up in a sort of untidy heap, snoring loudly.

It was a strange tree, the Queen was sure of it. When she had acquired it as a potted sapling, the tree had increased its height on the first day by a half. That was odd enough, but then on the second day its height had increased by a third, and on the third day its height had increased by a quarter, and so on and so on and so on.

The tree was now 100 times its original height and wouldn't fit in any of the rooms of the palace, not even the one with the squeaking floorboards and the really high ceiling. There was little else for it: she was going to have to invest in a roof window.

How many days had the Queen possessed the tree for?

Solution on page **140**

# SOUP DRAGON

## THE DUCHESS WAS THE USUAL TARGET
for the saucepans, plates and dishes that the Cook liked to throw around the kitchen. When the Queen of Hearts sent her to prison, however, the Cook was at a loss. Needing a new mark, the Cook directed her ire – and her fire-irons – at the hearth.

This was all fine in a destructive sort of way, until a rogue frying pan was lobbed out of her hand and into the fire, knocking the cauldron to the floor.

If ever there was a catastrophe, this probably wouldn't have been it, but if there were several catastrophes then it would certainly have merited a place in the discussion. When the Cook picked the cauldron up, peppery soup spilling everywhere, she saw that it was damaged beyond repair. After hurling a tureen at a windowsill, she headed to market.

The replacement cauldron and ladle that the Cook bought cost £45 in total, although she noted with a delicious frugal agony that the cauldron had cost £44 more than the ladle.

What was the price of each item individually?

Solution on page 140

# THEREFORE YOU'RE MAD

**THE CHESHIRE CAT** was trying to prove that Alice was mad, but she couldn't quite follow its logic. Perhaps this was a sign, she supposed, that it was right.

Alice had been asked to think of a number between one and twenty while the Cat did the same. Its argument was that if she thought of a higher number then she was most definitely mad, although it refused to explain why.

What is the probability that Alice's number is greater than the Cheshire Cat's?

Solution on page **141**

# MONKEY PUZZLE

**THIS FIENDISH PUZZLE** is perhaps the
most famous that Lewis Carroll devised,
and one he struggled to answer:
in a letter to a colleague he wrote
"It is a *most* puzzling puzzle."

A rope is hung over a pulley fixed to the roof of a building. On one end
of the rope is a monkey, which is exactly counterbalanced by a weight
hanging on the other end. Both the weight and the monkey are the
same distance from the pulley, and the rope and the pulley are both
weightless and frictionless.

If the monkey climbs the rope, what will be the result?

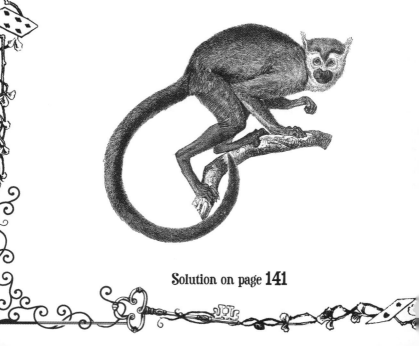

Solution on page 141

# WHAT ALICE FOUND THERE

## "KITTY, can you play chess? Now, don't smile, my dear, I'm asking it seriously."

Alice was sitting curled up in a corner of the great arm-chair, half talking to herself and half asleep. She had been trying for some time to coax her kitten into joining her for a game of chess, but her success in this pursuit had been limited.

Knowing that she was beaten, Alice decided to put the set away. As she grabbed the pouch for the chess pieces, she could feel that there was a pawn in there already, but had no idea whether it was red or white.

She had only managed to put a single white pawn into the pouch when she had an idea: she reached into the pouch, swirled the two pieces around with her fingers, and pulled one of them out. It was a white pawn.

What is now the chance of Alice drawing a white pawn from the pouch?

Adapted from *Pillow Problems* by Lewis Carroll

Solution on page 142

# HADDOCKS' EYES

### "THE PRETTIEST ARE ALWAYS FURTHER!" said Alice, sighing at the obstinacy of the rushes in growing so far off.

It seemed like nothing lovely was ever quite near enough. Alice rowed the boat steadily across the still pond, the Sheep continuing to knit furiously with an increasing number of needles. "How can she knit with so many?" the puzzled child thought. "She gets more and more like a porcupine every minute!"

She was distracted from this notion by a haddock, which breached the water directly in front of her. On a usual day the sight of a jumping haddock would have been just cause for bafflement, even wonder, but usual days rarely included rowboat trips with a knitting ovine.

Alice counted a dozen strokes of her oars until the boat first crossed the ever-widening circle made by the fish, and then another dozen before she broke through the circle on its opposite side.

How far away was the haddock at the moment it jumped?

Solution on page 143

# SOLUTIONS

# BISCUIT BUST UP

There were 15 biscuits on the tray.

The Hatter had 8 biscuits, The March Hare had 4 and the Dormouse had 2, leaving the last biscuit for Alice.

# OYSTERLINGS

All of the oysterlings are male.

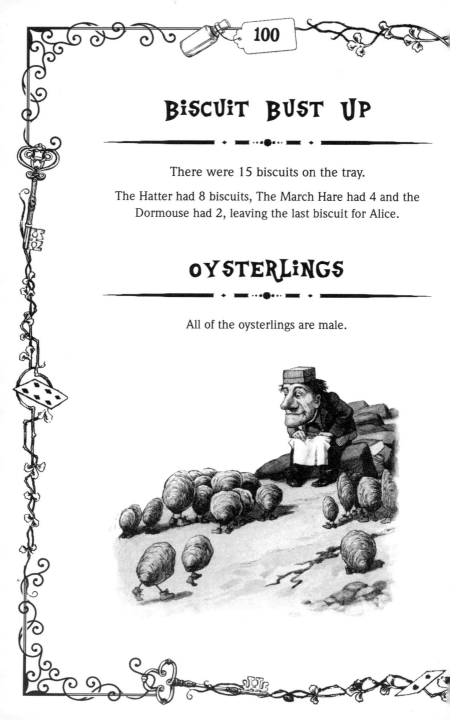

# DISEMBODIED VERSE

The answer is the word "Surface".

# AGAINST ALL ADVICE

The man warned the Goat about the 12:50 train because
it is ten to one (10 to 1) if you catch it.

# ENTOMOLOGICAL EQUATIONS

Alice was looking at four insects.

# FUSSY FELINE

The solution to this puzzle can be found by speaking it aloud.
Lewis Carroll gives the answer in verse:

*That salmon and sole Puss should think very grand*
*Is no such remarkable thing.*
*For more of these dainties Puss took up her stand;*
*But when the third sister stretched out her fair hand*
*Pray why should Puss swallow her ring?*

# BoXED iN

As a lecturer in mathematics Lewis Carroll loved mathematical and logic puzzles, but here he was being more literal. He gave the answer in verse:

*As curly-headed Jemmy was sleeping in bed,*
*His brother John gave him a blow on the head;*
*James opened his eyelids, and spying his brother,*
*Doubled his fist, and gave him another.*
*This kind of box then is not so rare;*
*The lids are the eyelids, the locks are the hair,*
*And so every schoolboy can tell to his cost,*
*The key to the tangles is constantly lost.*

# NoT THE QUiET CARRiAGE

The gentleman dressed in white paper is 30.

# FISH SUPPER

An oyster.

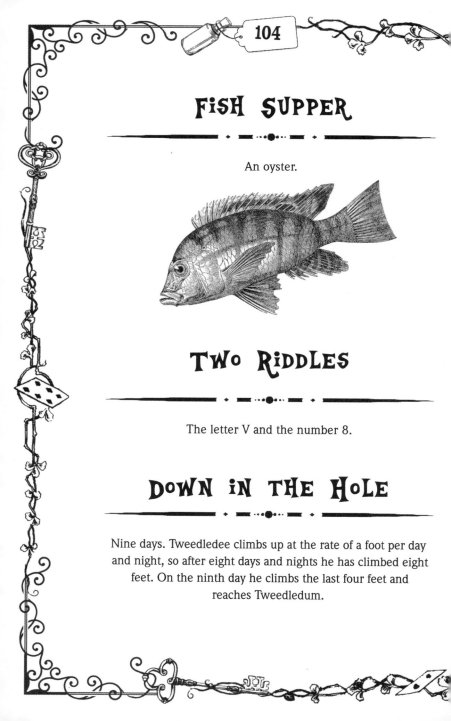

# TWO RIDDLES

The letter V and the number 8.

# DOWN IN THE HOLE

Nine days. Tweedledee climbs up at the rate of a foot per day and night, so after eight days and nights he has climbed eight feet. On the ninth day he climbs the last four feet and reaches Tweedledum.

# BUSHEL BUSINESS

There are ten apples on the wall.

# THE SNEEZING SALESMAN

The merchant ground a sack and a ninth for the Cook, which after taking a tenth as a toll would leave exactly one sack.

# PULLING THE OTHER ONE

Haigh was the strongest, followed by the Lion,
the Unicorn and then Hatta.

# AN AVERAGE FROG FAMILY

The Frog-Footman was 30. His brother was 32,
his sister was 36 and his mother was 58.

# A QUEENLY SUM

The answer is zero: anything multiplied by 0 is 0.

# DEAR DAIRY

The brown cows were the better milkers.

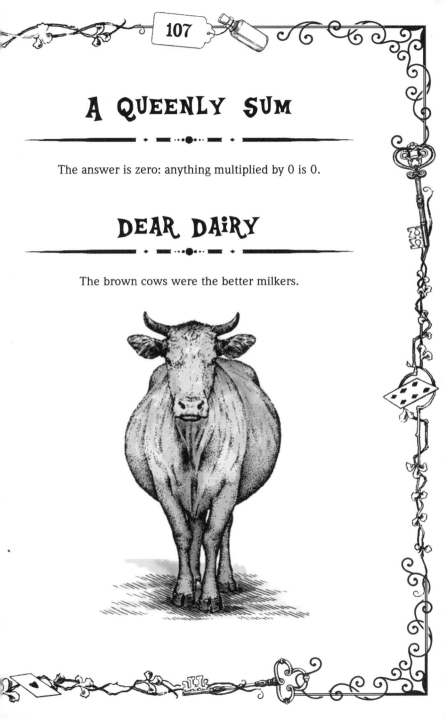

# FELINE FRUSTRATION

The answer is a tablet.

# A FACE-DOWN HAND

From left to right, the three playing cards are the Knave of Clubs, the Knave of Diamonds and the King of Diamonds.

# A GOOD EGG

The smallest possible number of eggs is 103, and the sheep sold 60 every day. Any multiple of these two will work, but we require the smallest possible numbers.

# PUTTING THEMSELVES TOGETHER

The probability is zero. If twelve of the riders found their own horse, then the thirteenth would have found theirs, too.

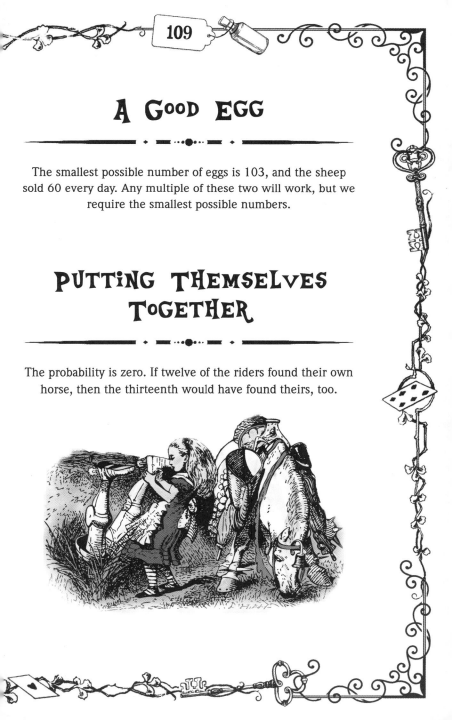

# LAWN FOR LUNCH

The animals will eat all of the grass in 40 days. As the cow and goat eat $\frac{1}{45}$ of the garden in a day, the cow and goose eat $\frac{1}{60}$ in a day and the goat and goose eat $\frac{1}{90}$ we can calculate that the cow eats $\frac{5}{360}$ of the garden in a day, the goat eats $\frac{3}{360}$ and the goose eats $\frac{1}{360}$. Therefore they eat $\frac{9}{360}$ of the garden in a day, or $\frac{1}{40}$.

# TIME TO REFLECT

The time correct to the nearest second was 27 minutes and 42 seconds after 6 o'clock.

# CATERING CONUNDRUM

It would take Haigh and Hatta 3½ minutes to fill a tray with twenty pieces of white and brown bread.

# A MOVING QUARRY

As Alice headed towards the White Rabbit, he walked backwards at the same pace.

# A Regal Runaround

The distance between the Looking Glass House and the Garden of Live Flowers is eleven miles.

# Out of Time

To get the real time, the number of minutes indicated on the watch must be deducted from 60. The time indicated would be exactly $23\frac{1}{13}$ minutes after four o'clock, but because the minute hand moves in the opposite direction, the real time would be $36\frac{12}{13}$ minutes after four o'clock.

# ABSENT HEDGEHOGS

Five forgot the hedgehogs.

# UNDER THE SEA

It wouldn't matter which building the Mock Turtle chose:
all three paths would be the same length. The length isn't
determined by the building's shape but by the slope of the road.
As they all have the same slope, their paths are the same length
from their bases to their tops.

# BRANDY BOTHER

As both tumblers have ended up containing 50 spoonfuls of liquid, the quantities transferred are identical: $^{50}/_{51}$ of brandy was moved from the first tumbler to the second and $^{50}/_{51}$ of water was moved from the second tumbler to the first.

**Note:** this solution is the mathematically correct one, but doesn't take into account the molecules of water and alcohol that are occupied in certain volumes of pure solutions of the other.

# FULL LEISURELY WE GLIDE

Fifty-two times. Dum and Dee (the first and next boy, although if you call them this aloud they'll get angry) row to the right bank, and then one of them brings the boat back. One soldier rows across, and the boy on the right bank brings the boat back.

This means it takes four crossings to get a soldier across. The whole process is repeated twelve times (fifty-two crossings) to get the King and his twelve men across, leaving Tweedledee and Tweedledum with their boat.

# ROYALLY AFRAID

"I am notable; I am no table; I am not able."

# FOOTLOOSE FOOTMAN

The Fish-Footman worked for 6 days and idled for 24.
He was paid £240 in total for the 30 days, and had to forfeit
£240 for the days he wasted.

# TIME TRADES

The tea-party is happening at 2 p.m. on Thursday.

# MISSING OUT

*When Mary and Ina told Hartie they'd seen a*
*Small creature with wings, dressed in crimson and blue,*
*Hartie cried "'Twas a fairy! Why, Ina and Mary,*
*I should have been happy if I had been you!"*
*Said Mary "You wouldn't." Said Ina "You shouldn't –*
*Since you can't be us, and we couldn't be you.*
*You are one, my dear Hartie, but we are a party,*
*And arithmetic tells us that one isn't two."*

# SEEING RED (OR GREY)

The figure's second statement covers both colours, which means it must be telling the truth. It is therefore the Red Castle.

# THE WILLIAMS

The ages are as follows: Father William, 39; Noah, 21; Arthur, 18; John, 18; Joyce, 12; Phyllis, 9. Arthur and John are twins.

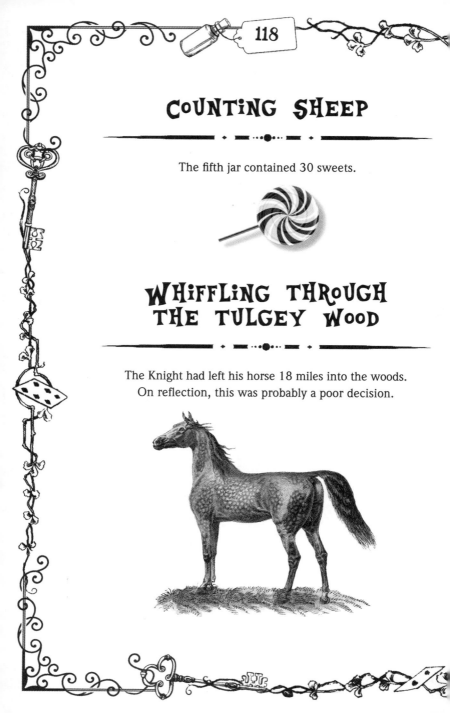

# COUNTING SHEEP

The fifth jar contained 30 sweets.

# WHIFFLING THROUGH THE TULGEY WOOD

The Knight had left his horse 18 miles into the woods. On reflection, this was probably a poor decision.

# SECOND GUESSING

The word is "Wholesome".

# PENAL PUZZLE

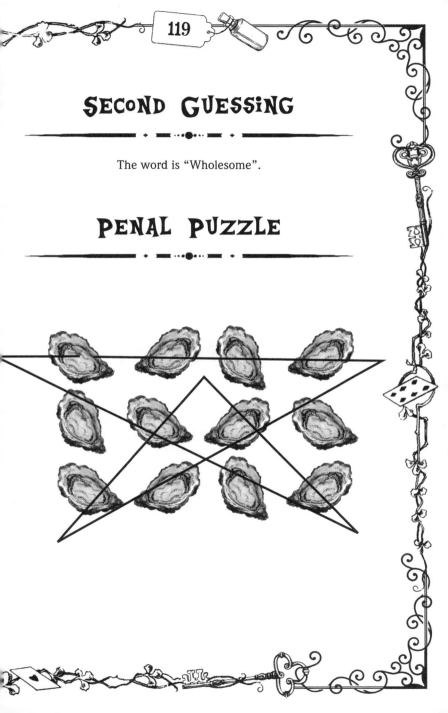

# Midway on Her Journey

Alice should take the first path. If the second or third path is the correct choice, all three finger-posts are true, while if the first path is correct, then all three finger-posts are false.

# Wine Not?

The White Queen, Red Queen and White Knight poured the contents of two of the half-full casks into two of the other half-full casks. This created nine full casks, nine empty casks and three half-full casks. They could each then take three full and three empty casks and one half-full cask.

# Yolkfolk

Daisy is thirty and Denzil is twelve.

# Something to Dunk

The Hatter ate 213 biscuits a week. From the 160 biscuits he bought he made 40 more, and from those 10 he made another two, plus two ends left over. From those last two biscuits he made two ends to add to the two ends he already had, producing one final biscuit. That last biscuit made one more end, which he kept for the following week, presumably hidden under his hat or the sleeping head of the Dormouse.

# Discriminating Descendants

Father William had ten children.

# A FAWN FEIGNING INTEREST

The word is "Envelope".

# LIKE A FRIEND

Neither Tweedledum nor Tweedledee had any friends:
zero times two remains zero. They had each other, at least.

# Running Up That Hill

It was 6¾ miles to the top of the hill; Alice ascended in 4½ hours and descended in 1½ hours.

# Leaving the Nest

It was her seventh birthday.

# SUNLESS SARTORIAL SELECTIONS

Five socks. In the worst scenario the King would remove four socks of a different colour, meaning that the fifth one would have to create a matching pair.

# No BALL GAMES

Bill threw the ball straight up into the air.

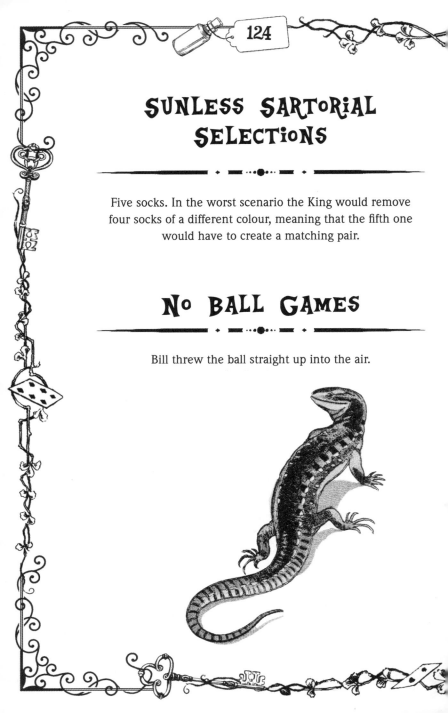

# RECIPROCAL ZUGZWANG

The White Knight had won three rounds and the Red Knight had won two rounds.

**Note:** Zugzwang is a situation in chess where the obligation to move puts the player at a disadvantage. As both Knights are so roundly incompetent that they frequently tumble off their own horses, their clashes are an example of reciprocal zugzwang.

# ON THE PAYROLL

Haigh's deal was better. During the first year, Hatta receives £300 and Haigh receives £330 (£150 + £150 + £30.) During the second year Hatta receives £360 (£300 + £60) and Haigh receives £450 (£180 + £30 + £210 + £30). At this point Haigh has already earned £120 more than Hatta, and will receive increasingly more as the years progress.

# Sea Legs

The Caterpillar's question can't be answered. The water won't reach the top rung: as the ship will rise with the tide, the water will remain at the same level as the bottom rung.

# Field Surgery

The three fractions were 40/60 for black eyes, 45/60 for sprained wrists and 48/60 for stubbed toes. Add together 40, 55 and 28 and deduct twice 60 and the result is 13, the minimum number for every 60 patients. As the minimum who could have sustained all three injuries was 26, the number of injured soldiers must have been 120.

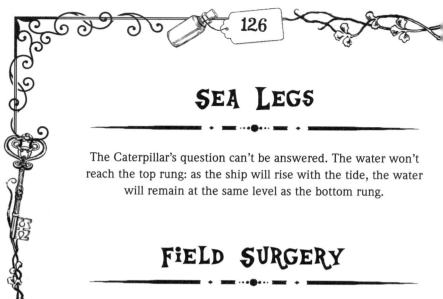

# DRAUGHTY CONDITIONS

There were 10 games played. Each of the five passengers played four other passengers, like so:

# FAIRLY REDISTRIBUTED WEALTH

Each boy starts with 3p and gives 1p to every girl. Each girl starts with 15p and gives 2p to every boy. Each child then has 6p.

# i AM THE EGG MAN

The King travelled roughly 96½ miles (96.568 miles, to be precise). This figure is the square root of twice the square of 40, added to 40.

# i AM THE WALRUS

The Walrus ate no oysters on Monday. He then ate three on Tuesday, six on Wednesday, nine on Thursday and a dozen on the Friday, making thirty in total.

# PiLLoW PRoBLEMS

The Russian's third son is called Yvan. Their names relate to their professions: Rab is "bar" backwards, Ymra is "army" and Yvan is "navy".

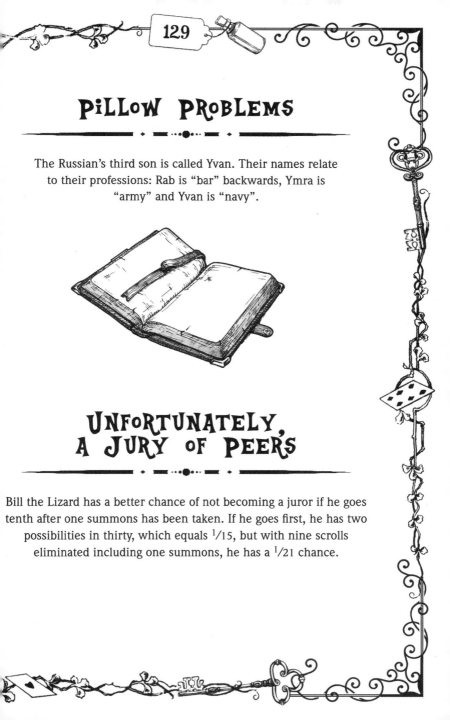

# UNFoRTUNATELY, A JURY oF PEERS

Bill the Lizard has a better chance of not becoming a juror if he goes tenth after one summons has been taken. If he goes first, he has two possibilities in thirty, which equals $1/15$, but with nine scrolls eliminated including one summons, he has a $1/21$ chance.

## SALT iRE

Alice could put four of the sacks on either side of the scale.
If they didn't balance, she'd know that the salt was among those on
the heavier side of the scale. If they did balance, she'd know that
the salt was in the four that she didn't weigh.

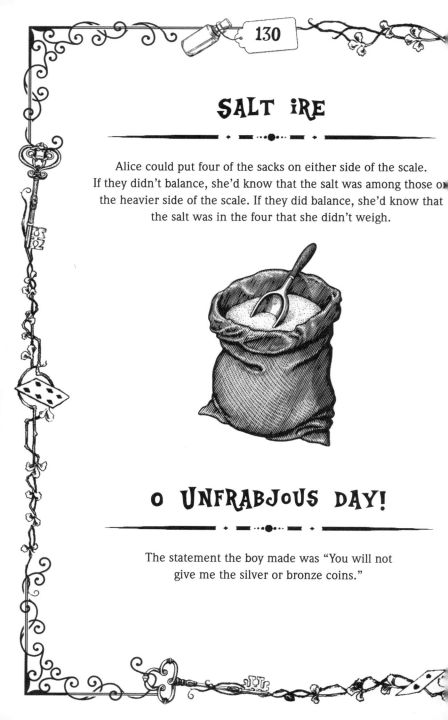

## O UNFRABJOUS DAY!

The statement the boy made was "You will not
give me the silver or bronze coins."

# IMPROPER WAGON MAINTENANCE

The King had sent 900 soldiers in all. 100 wagons set off with 9 soldiers in each. After 10 broke down, there were 10 in each wagon. As 15 more were withdrawn, each of the remaining 75 wagons carried 12 soldiers, which is 3 more than when they had started out.

# RACE FOR THE PRIZE

The Eaglet would pass the Lory in $6^2/3$ minutes.

# TROUBLE AND A HALF

The answer is half a hen plus half a hen, or one hen: if one and a half hens lay one and a half eggs in one and a half days, one hen will lay one egg in one and a half days. A hen who lays better by half will lay one and a half eggs in one and a half days (one egg per day). Therefore, one hen will lay ten and a half eggs (half a score and a half) in ten and a half days (a week and a half).

# OKAY AT CROQUET

Five was the Doorward, Two was the Cup-Bearer, Four was the Dapifer and Six was the Pantler.

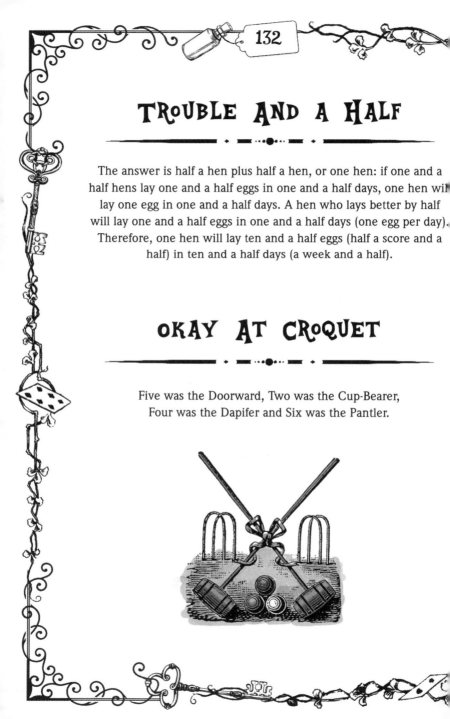

# THERE GOES THE SUN

The summer holidays had been going on for 18 days, or 19 if you include the current day (which you had been explicitly asked not to, but fine).

# CURSED BE LOVE!

The poem is a square: if you read it vertically, starting with the first word of the first line and continuing on to the first word of the second line, you will see the exact same poem as if you had read it horizontally.

# CRUEL AND UNUSUAL PUNISHMENTS

Hatta should put one red marble in one of the jars and the remaining 199 marbles in the other. This gives him a 74.87% chance of being released.

The probability of selecting either jar is 0.5, the probability of drawing a red marble from one jar is 1 and from the other jar is 99/199. Therefore the overall probability is
$$0.5 \times (1) + 0.5 \times (99/199) = 0.7487.$$

# GUEST AT THE FEAST

There were 60 guests. This solution can be worked out with a few equations:

$$\frac{x}{2} + \frac{x}{3} + \frac{x}{4} = 65$$

Therefore:

$$6x + 4x + 3x = 65 \times 12$$

$$13x = 65 \times 12$$

$$x = 60$$

# INTERGENERATIONAL CRAB CATCHING

There were just three people in the boat: a grandfather, his son and his grandson. Two of the three were fathers and two of the three were sons.

# A PIECE OF CAKE

With her first two cuts Alice divided the cake into quarters, then she brought the knife to the side of the cake and sliced it horizontally.

# Without a Full Deck

The aged aged man had a better chance of winning. After drawing one ace (and returning it) he would have a 4 in 52 (or 1 in 13) chance of drawing a second ace. The White Knight, on the other hand (having discarded the first ace), would now have a 3 in 51 (or 1 in 17) chance with his second turn.

# A Lying Leporine

Alice could ask the March Hare "Is today either Monday or Wednesday?" If it was a Monday the Hare would correctly answer yes, if it was a Tuesday it would incorrectly answer yes, if it was a Wednesday it would incorrectly answer no, and if it was a Thursday it would correctly answer no (it couldn't have been a Friday, Saturday or Sunday).

This means that if the Hare answers yes it is hosting a tea-party, and if it answers no it is going to a tea-party.

# PASTRY PREMONITIONS

Four was the nightwatchman – by telling the Queen about his dream, he'd exposed himself as being asleep on the job.

# OUT ON THE TILES

The soot line crosses 321 tiles. Alice's diagonal line enters a new tile at the beginning and each time it crosses a horizontal or vertical line. However, when the soot crosses the corner of a tile it is crossing two lines but only entering one tile. These corners are corners of rectangles proportional to the whole floor; the diagonals of such rectangles are on the main diagonal. The number of such rectangles equals the greatest common divisor of 231 and 93, which is 3. The whole floor is included as such a rectangle, since the diagonal, reaching its end, does not enter a new tile. The sum therefore is $231 + 93 - 3$, which equals 321.

# AN EVOLUTIONARY CUL-DE-SAC

20 per cent. To work this out, let's say for example that there were 100 Bread-and-butter-flies. As the number of Bread-and-butter-flies is 25 per cent of the number of other insects, that would make 400 insects that weren't Bread-and-butter-flies. The total number of insects would therefore be 100 + 400 = 500, which makes them 100/500 insects, or a fifth, which is 20 per cent.

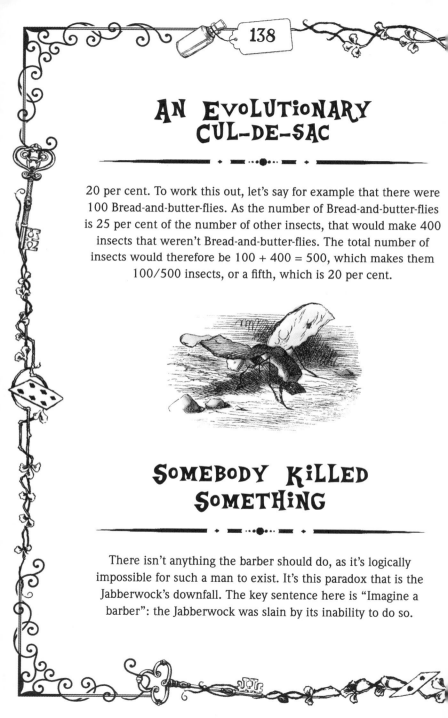

# SOMEBODY KILLED SOMETHING

There isn't anything the barber should do, as it's logically impossible for such a man to exist. It's this paradox that is the Jabberwock's downfall. The key sentence here is "Imagine a barber": the Jabberwock was slain by its inability to do so.

# A Flipper With A Hand

The Walrus and the Carpenter played nine hands of the card game. First, the Carpenter won three hands, winning three pennies. The Walrus then won the three pennies back with another three hands, and finally the Carpenter won a three further hands to win the sum total of three pennies, or vice versa.

# Blind Chance

$1/24$. The first card has a one in four chance of getting to their original corner, the second card has one in three chances, the third card has one in two chances and the last has one in one. The sum to work this out is therefore: $\frac{1}{4} \times \frac{1}{3} \times \frac{1}{2} \times \frac{1}{1} = \frac{1}{24}$.

# TUMTUM TREE TROUBLES

The Queen had possessed the tree for 198 days. If, for example, it was a metre tall when bought, then on the end of the first day it would be 1½ metres tall. On the next day it would gain a third of 1½ m (½ m), making it 2 metres tall, and on the day after that it would gain a quarter of 2 metres (also ½ m). This means it would gain ½ m each day. After 198 days it would have gained 99 metres, which would make it 100 times as tall as on the first day.

# SOUP DRAGON

The cauldron cost £44.50 and the ladle cost 50p.

# THEREFORE YOU'RE MAD

The probability that Alice's number is greater is 19 out of 40. The chances that both numbers are the same is 1 out of 20, which means the probability that they're different is 19 out of 20. If they're different, then the chances are even that Alice's number is higher, so the total probability is one half of 19 out of 20, which is also 19 out of 40. It turned out, though, that Alice and the Cheshire Cat thought of the exact same number. The Cat also took this result as proof: "Because I'm mad, you see, so if you weren't mad then you wouldn't have thought of the same thing as me." It was difficult to argue with the logic.

# MONKEY PUZZLE

Regardless of how the monkey climbs, the weight and the monkey always stay at the same level.

# WHAT ALICE FOUND THERE

The solution to this puzzle is counter-intuitive. It would appear at first sight that the pouch is in an identical state after Alice removes the first pawn as before she put it in, with a 1 in 2 chance of a white pawn. This, however, is an error.

There are three possibilities that will result in Alice putting a white pawn in the pouch and taking out a white pawn:

1. The pouch originally contained a white pawn and Alice removes this white pawn.

2. The pouch originally contained a red pawn and Alice removes the white pawn she put in.

3. The pouch originally contained a white pawn and Alice removes the white pawn she put in.

Two of these three equally likely outcomes involve a white pawn staying in the pouch, so the chances of Alice drawing a white pawn again are 2 in 3.

# HADDOCKS' EYES

The fish was sixteen strokes away when it jumped.

# ALSO AVAILABLE:

*Alice's Puzzles in Wonderland*
ISBN: 978-1-78097-675-4